When God Sends an Angel

When God Sends an Angel

Gay Nicol

iUniverse, Inc.
New York Lincoln Shanghai

When God Sends an Angel

iUniverse books may be ordered through booksellers or by contacting:

iUniverse
2021 Pine Lake Road, Suite 100
Lincoln, NE 68512
www.iuniverse.com
1-800-Authors (1-800-288-4677)

ISBN-13: 978-0-595-41502-1 (pbk)
ISBN-13: 978-0-595-85851-4 (ebk)
ISBN-10: 0-595-41502-4 (pbk)
ISBN-10: 0-595-85851-1 (ebk)

Printed in the United States of America

Soon after the loss of my precious four year old granddaughter, Maddie, in the middle of one night I sat up in bed; and the words (When God Sends An Angel) penetrated my heart and mind with such force that it made me aware that I had a task to accomplish. I had a story, and it was one that certainly should be told. I must not retreat from the responsibility. The problem, however, with my story was where do I begin? As a Latin teacher of many years, a famous Latin quote randomly came to mind "In Medias Res," translated in the middle of things. I decided to begin my story right there in the middle of things.

Being a single mother of two daughters, Valory and Laura, and obviously working hard as a teacher and provider for my girls, I suddenly began having Asthma attacks on a regular basis. My age was not helping the detriment occurring to my lungs, and my pulmonary doctor informed me that a forced retirement was fast approaching. I was devastated; for I loved teaching teenagers Latin, but the doctor stated that I was enveloped too much by ill health not to be affected adversely. So I began the retirement process which was so inundated with bureaucracy that I barely met the deadlines for my pending retirement. I had also, months earlier, begun the building of my new retirement home in Lexington, Kentucky where both of my daughters and their families were now residing. My oldest daughter, Valory, had a little girl named Regan who was one year old. My other daughter, Laura, had a son named Taylor who was three years old; and with excitement she was expecting the arrival of her second child, predicted to be a little girl. So the disappointment with my early retirement was quickly being replaced with all my anticipation of focusing on my own precious children and grandchildren. My daughter, Laura, had delivered her second child who was an adorable little girl named Maddie.

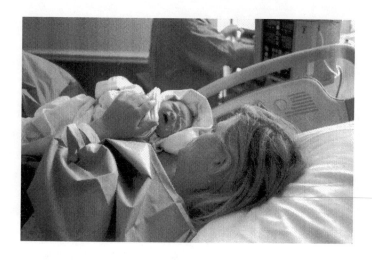

From the beginning a special bond

She was beautiful and perfect in every way. My life had never been happier. I said farewell to a career that had provided me with the most inspiring life and a tremendous feeling of fulfillment. As I left that meaningful facility, where I had taught and learned from one teenager after another, I did not look back. Somehow I knew that I would never return, and that my life was changing far more than I would have ever imagined.

Four days after my retirement, my sister and I had taken my mother to her summer home in Florida. We had only been there two days when I received a phone call from my daughter, Laura, saying; "Mom you must come here immediately! Something is wrong with Maddie. She keeps leaning to the left when she is sitting up," for Maddie was now ten months old. My daughter was such a wonderful mother, and I knew that she was very sensitive to every aspect of her children. Sensing urgency, my mother, sister and I packed and returned to Atlanta; and then I drove to Kentucky.

Maddie was still laughing her precious raucous laugh; and until just recently she was nursing all the time, which had led to my nicknaming her snack pack; and she was playing like any healthy child would be doing.

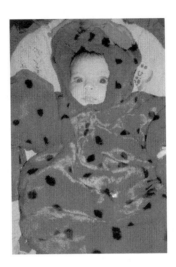

Halloween doesn't get cuter

I dare you!

I don't think I have arrived

However, her mom was now placing a pillow behind her back because she had lost the ability to sit in one day. Her doctor ordered an MRI, and we all prayed and then shouted and cheered when the clinic called back, "All looked fine". It was a very temporary relief because her irritability began escalating and her comfort diminished. Seven days later another heartbreaking loss occurred when Maddie discovered she could not raise her thumb to her mouth. She then could no longer suck, and she was experiencing difficulty in swallowing some things. She would look at her thumb and cry because she was frustrated with these gruesome changes that she was experiencing. An NG tube had been inserted as a temporary solution for her nutritional loss and dehydration. Her brother, Taylor, so badly wanted the NG tube removed when he saw his little sister. Her regression continued leaving us devastated and fearful as we tried to find answers knowing we were losing her one day at a time. My daughter and I began the search for a doctor who could diagnose this dreadful occurrence. We first sought help locally; and then still with no answers, we went to Cincinnati Children's Hospital and checked in through the ER. We already had an appointment scheduled with the neurology team in Cincinnati, but it was months away. We had informed the insurance company while in route what we were doing. After all the multitude of paperwork was filled out, we were situated in a holding room that was designed with huge glass windows for observation purpose. My daughter and I were frolicking and trying to entertain Maddie; and her little tickle box got turned over, and she laughed so hard with the most infectious laugh, that when we looked up there were people everywhere gathering and enjoying every aspect of this beautiful and innocent little girl.

Life doesn't get any funnier than Taylor

That same day in Cincinnati the doctors delivered the diagnosis after comparing the Lexington MRI scan and the one that they had taken. Their faces reflected the tragedy that they knew they had to divulge, and my daughter and I knew that we were about to hear words that would change who we were and what we must have the strength to do in order that our precious Maddie experience as much of the beauty of this world as possible. We also wanted her to be shared because every life has a valuable purpose to fulfill before moving on to the life God had originally planned for mankind.

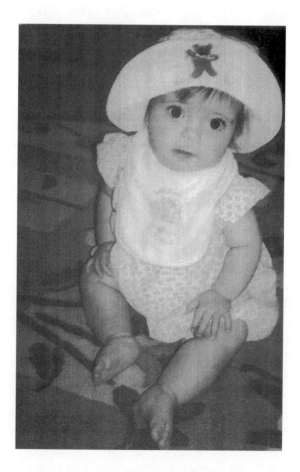

Everybody wants to take me home

We both realized that the only way we could persevere with what was ahead was with God as our strength, being in total control, and trusting that he had a perfect plan. Fortunately we had that faith. Maddie's diagnosis was one of the Leukodystrophies which is a regressive neurological disease that is terminal. While we were there, the hospital also provided a genetic counselor. Now it was a wait and see for the final diagnosis as to which Leukodystrophy Maddie had. Within a few days, the phone rang; and Laura answered with her hand shaking, and I heard her say, "No, please tell me now on the phone. I cannot drive to Cincinnati." The genetic counselor reluctantly told Laura that it was Krabbe, the very worst and most lupine of all the Leukodystrophies. It is also the most painful. I stood and watched life flow from my daughter as she said, Oh No!!! Naturally she had lived on the internet since the inception of Maddie's decline, and now her worst nightmare was true. She knew exactly what Krabbe was and the devastation that it would impose hourly, daily, but certainly not yearly. Her diagnosis was that Maddie would never experience her second birthday.

One of the members of the team did suggest that Laura take Maddie to Duke where there was a doctor who was a specialist in the Krabbe disease. If the disease was not too advanced there might be a possibility of a cord blood transplant. The doctor at Duke expressed a willingness to see Maddie as quickly as possible; but even before the rushed up journey began, Maddie became very ill; and her regression took hold again. She barely made the journey to Duke. After close examination her doctor sat Maddie's mom and dad down and said, "If it was my child, I would not do the transplant. It is of my opinion that she would not live through the transplant process. Any damage already present could not be reversed."

I see you!

My daughter and I decided at least to stay at Duke and get Maddie's feeding tube and nissen wrap surgery. Then we would spend the necessary time for the team of doctors to observe Maddie and arrive at her medicinal needs to limit the unpredictable destruction and suffering of this disease. Laura and I stayed a month at Duke, and the first course of action was the feeding tube and nissen wrap (to prevent reflux and aspiration) surgery. After the surgery, no pain medication relieved Maddie's pain, including Morphine. She awoke from the surgery moving her little mouth like she was nursing, and I have never felt such helplessness and irresolvable pain in my life. I knew that precious baby was just grieving for the bond she and her mother had shared that had produced nothing short of real contentment, security, and happiness. My little snack pack was dreaming of nursing throughout her whole surgery, I am certain.

If it just doesn't sting

Because of her pain and need for comfort, they agreed to let her mother spend the night in Maddie's hospital room; but only one person was allowed. Well, this is where I began to see a tigress grandmother come out in me. I was not about to leave, so I slept in the tub in the accompanying bathroom. The good news was that I was not born a basketball player standing seven feet tall, but it would have been perfect had I been born a dwarf. We persevered and even brought laughter to those who caught Laura's and my singing with The Wiggles around Maddie's bed and dancing to entertain our little Angel. Our next hurdle resulted from the pain Maddie experienced when we fed her; so I went out and bought all these singing and dancing animal toys to hold her attention while we did a feeding. One of the animals was a bulldog that sang, Who Let The Dogs Out; and then it barked. Well, we were turned in for having a dog in our hotel room. In the middle of sadness you can always find laughter; and in the middle of ugliness you can always find beauty. I continued to observe this throughout our journey with our cherished little Maddie Mae. With the feeding tube in place and the feedings begun, our next obstacle was that Maddie was not tolerating the formula. She began vomiting; and then diarrhea ensued, so we rushed her back to the hospital. I have never seen so many doctors trying to find an answer. Computers were cranking out the names of formulas one after another. Finally, one doctor found a formula totally unfamiliar but with much possibility as an answer. This formula was predigested; and from Maddie's first encounter with this formula she responded in a positive way, and that never changed. That was to be her nutrition until her final moment: all of this because of the care and concern of another human being, and that would become one of my many memories of human goodness that surfaces in the face of adversity.

Now we had Maddie's nutritional needs met, but she continued having to tolerate much pain. Laura and I would take turns strolling her back and forth in out hotel room all night, which calmed her somewhat. The pain, however, was escalating as her fragile little body was being devoured with this horrendous disease. We would wait for many hours just to see her doctor because the entire staff was so overworked trying to save these children or stave off the attack of this formidable disease. Maddie's doctor finally figured out that Methadone would relieve her pain, but I believe only a few other Krabbe children had been prescribed Methadone for pain before. It would take several months for the Methadone to become totally effective. Maddie had also developed Stryder while we were there. Stryder is a terrible noise accompanying each breath; and it was the result of Maddie's nervousness and insecurities with these downward spiraling, acrimonious transitions she was trying to endure. The doctor diagnosed Ativan for that symptom. We left knowing we could call our Duke team for other medications as the disease progressed. Our trip home was arduous; and Laura and I were drained, and we could see in everyone's expressions the horror of Maddie's decline in one month. Just in one month, she had lost all neuromuscular control; and when Laura picked her up and brought her into the house, she looked like a little rag doll. I had to stay back; for copious tears were overflowing my eyes, and I felt a pain that I thought I would not be able to endure. Once again, however, God lifted me up to arise to my responsibilities and not to succumb to my human frailties. Laura situated Maddie on a mattress on the ground floor of their home, so Hospice could deliver Maddie's equipment and demonstrate to Laura the procedures necessary to operate. She had oxygen, and a suction machine, and a feeding machine and an albuterol machine for breathing treatments. From this point on, I was privileged to observe my daughter, Laura, manifest a miracle from God in her ability to care for Maddie with a love and determination that created in this lifeless child the same determination as her mother's. Maddie was choosing a life abundant, needing nothing but love. This is when I discovered life's most valuable lesson, the one common ingredient necessary for quality life or life at all is love.

Love poured out for all the world to see

My Gagee would rock me all day if my mommy would let her

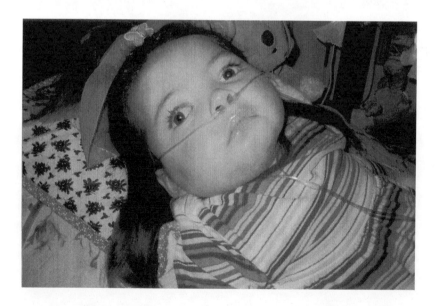

My mother has her own beauty pageant going...local

Laura and I both slept downstairs with Maddie. We bought a single mattress which we placed in alignment with Maddie's, and then we used the sofa. We alternated the feedings and medications throughout the night. Whoever was sleeping next to Maddie held her hand because that was how we could tell that she needed to be suctioned. The disease manifests itself with different symptoms. Maddie mainly had the problem of thick secretions accompanied with an inability to swallow. I am sure that this was frightening to her because her little hand would start shaking uncontrollably when the secretions were filling her throat. We would jump up and suction her quickly. We kept the suction machine right next to her. Sometimes the secretions were so thick that they would get infected and leave her vulnerable to pneumonia. Therefore, a medicine was added to ameliorate this problem; and now Hospice was added to what eventually became a team of caregivers, each one completely dedicated to enhancing Maddie's life.

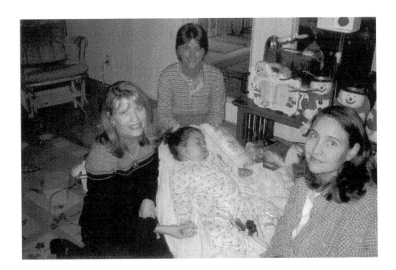

These ladies understand love

Hospice also assigned a main nurse in charge of Maddie's total healthcare; and from that point on she determined necessary medicinal changes or additions, and she was the one that was responsible for giving us the encouragement and confidence to embrace the love and beauty of our little Maddie Mae and not the disease. What a gift she gave us!!! The opportunity to enjoy every second of our blessing with this God sent angel.

One night when it was my shift to suction, check on her feeding to see that it was being absorbed, and to put her prepared medicines in her tube (Her mother always prepared all of her medicines. That was a crucial responsibility.); I was kneeling and looking into Maddie's beautiful face; and she was awake and looking at me, and I said, "Maddie, I Love You," and I blinked my eyes on the words I Love You. She blinked her eyes back three times, and I knew that God was sharing with me an unsurpassable miracle. We would be able to exchange with words and blinks our love and feelings for one another and even to develop further communication, and we did. We even filmed Maddie talking with her eyes in response to us, and her funny Easter bunny toy, and her birthday dog, and many other times including a TV interview on Newborn Screening that featured diseases similar to Maddie's disease. She blinked her eyes twice "yes" when her mother asked her if she was special. Then her mother asked Taylor, Maddie's five year old brother, if he wanted to tell his little sis that he loved her. Laura said, "She will tell you in any event," and Maddie batted her eyes three times with the camera on a close up shot. Once again, it was like previewing a little bit of heaven just watching Maddie's special way of expressing herself, and others being so moved by sharing in her special gifts. It is not the number of years that we live. It is the meaningfulness of those years that will ultimately make a difference in this world. A domino effect of the goodness in people continued throughout Maddie's life and is still continuing.

Again Maddie's regression ensued before she reached a plateau of her symptoms. During her difficult times, which escalated always in the winter, Laura became so aware and knowledgeable about Krabbe that she could recognize symptoms of infections or other complications before doctors and tests validated what Laura had already diagnosed. She was truly Maddie's most valuable advocate.

Urinary tract infections all of a sudden presented a problem, and so Laura consulted with her Hospice nurse about the possibility of Laura's catherizing Maddie four times every 24 hours. That became the next procedure along with alternating two different antibiotics every month. After this procedure was in place the urinary tract infections ceased. There were many other problems that Laura solved because no one in Lexington was familiar with Krabbe. Maddie's clothes had to be selected so carefully, so they would not cause any pressure that could culminate into bed sores. Dresses, for example, would tend to form wrinkles over a period of time that might cause pressure sores. Also dressing our little Angel took much patience and care because she would shake all over with the movements of her limbs, and so we had to select pants easy to slip on and tops that would slip over her head with easy access to her arms. She had no control of her body at all. We were constantly hunting and changing her wardrobe ideas to accomplish good health care but also to keep her a fashion statement for all to enjoy. She always looked so beautiful. She was the reflection of God's love.

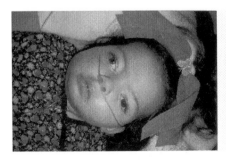 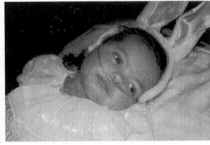

...State...   **...and National**

Her mother washed and coiffed her hair complete with ribbons or other adornments. Her nails were always polished, and she was always so clean that her fragrance was that of spring flowers.

The children in the neighborhood would periodically quit playing and come and sit by Maddie and enjoy her. I think Maddie evoked love and compassion from these children seeing her life so imperfect, and yet Maddie so loved life.

Life is sweet!

My mom and I bought Maddie a hot tub, and her physical therapist would work with her quite often in the hot tub. You could tell how much Maddie enjoyed that weightless feeling of her limbs, and the warmth of the water, and the movement of her body which she could not accomplish. The therapist loved Maddie, and Maddie always talked to her with her eyes. When asked, "does this feel good Maddie?" She would always blink twice. We filmed this also because we knew someday, when we had to say goodbye, that we would need every tool possible for recalling our short time with our treasured Angel. But as a matter of fact, what Laura and I learned after Maddie returned to God was that we wanted to share her abundant gifts from heaven. Laura decided to become a pediatric nurse, loving and caring for babies; and I continued to work with teenagers, not only as a Latin teacher, but also as someone to uplift their awareness of their value as individual human beings.

I think one of the last losses that Maddie confronted was the loss of her ability to smile, and what a smile she had! We had her first year pictures made right before one of the most beautiful visions on this earth, "Maddie's smile," succumbed to a dreadful disease. Maddie's smile was no more, except you could still find it in her eyes. The day of the pictures my job was to make her smile. Well, she used to always laugh at her brother, Taylor. Laura would call me long distance when I was still living in Atlanta to share with me the joy of Maddie's laughter at Taylor. She just could not quit laughing when he was entertaining her. I would sleep great after listening to that adored baby, so easily and totally enjoying her life. Taylor, of course, had to be in the family pictures; so I came prepared to get a smile from Maddie, one last smile; and I did by blowing up balloons and letting them go making this horrific noise. I think Maddie was the only one enjoying my antics, and everyone else was ready to strangle me. We did get a picture with her smile.

Laura prepared a great first year birthday party, and so many people attended. I pushed Maddie around in her stroller so that everyone could share with her in this special event.

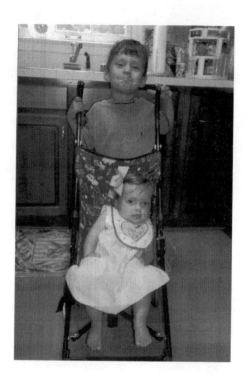

Come on Taylor, everybody wants to see me! I'm one

Our friends selected the most appropriate and enjoyable gifts for Maddie, and you could feel the love from all their thoughtfulness in their selections. The winter following Maddie's first birthday brought illnesses and trips to the hospital as we feared it would. It took two people to transport Maddie anywhere, because one person had to drive and the other had to sit in the middle seat in the van to suction her. It required many items to prepare for a car sojourn. We had to bring an oxygen canister, feedings, medicines, and the suction machine and her pulse ox machine to monitor her oxygen level. That winter we made a couple of trips to the hospital, but there was never a clear diagnosis of pneumonia—Praise The Lord! Throughout Maddie's four short years we made many trips to the hospital; but now in retrospect, those trips served as Maddie's continuing her gift to this world. Always by the time we left the hospital, she had endeared herself to everyone and revealed to those around her how a little girl, who had no visible reason to embrace life, could courageously continue to demonstrate her determination to experience love as long as possible.

As Maddie was growing physically, Laura and I felt it was now time to implement routine activities for her intellectual and spiritual growth. We used CD music and a Video Now to help her embrace life. We had a table next to her bed always displayed with different visual stimulations such as, a fish tank or lava lamps, and a butterfly mobile hanging from the ceiling.

My brother watches over me always

Every morning when she was most alert, before her AM medicines and after the effect of the PM medicines had subsided, I would sit next to Maddie and sing a routine of five songs which she loved; but everyone else tried to escape the experience. Her mother would walk through the room and say, "I am so sorry Maddie." I always began our song experience with GOOD MORNING TO YOU; and the last line is I REALLY DO LOVE YOU, and she would bat her eyes three times for I Love You. Our second song I will not share because I made it up; but she loved it, and that was all that mattered. The other grandchildren still sing it, and my heart aches. Our third song was JESUS LOVES YOU, and she batted those big beautiful eyes all the way through that one. The next song was YOU ARE MY SUNSHINE, and the last was FIVE LITTLE DUCKS WENT OUT TO PLAY. I had a hand puppet duck that quacked; and so when we got to the part where the mother duck said quack, quack, quack and five little ducks came waddling back; I of course would make the duck puppet quack, quack, quack. I purchased many other puppets, and we had many other puppet shows. I used a mirror every morning after she was bathed and coiffed and dressed by her mother, and I showed her how beautiful she looked. I would say, "Maddie, do you want to see the outfit that you are wearing today????" She would bat her eyes twice. With her bats, God's gift completely changed our lives from feeling hopeless and separated, to feeling blessed; from living in sadness to praising God for all the joy that we were experiencing and thanking him for trusting us to care for Maddie.

Laura would read to Maddie all the time, and she would point out the characters and tell Maddie all the colors and other elements in the stories. You could just watch Maddie's understanding of language and life and love expand. Maddie could even blink her eyes twice to let you know if she needed to be suctioned. We were truly walking in faith and enjoying all of the meaningful blessings that were occurring.

As Maddie continued to flourish, yet another person joined the team; and she was one whom Maddie also loved and responded to. She was a massage therapist, but she always went way beyond the description of her job. She was so soothing and used oils and creams that kept Maddie's skin so supple and healthy. During one visit, she had told us that her outlet for expressing her own feelings and emotions was belly dancing. She wanted us to come to the Greek restaurant where she preformed. We never experienced her dancing before she moved to San Diego. She was anxious about leaving Maddie, and we did have to let her know soon after her departure that Maddie now had her wings and was with her father in heaven. Maddie's therapist did return to see her headstone and share in special moments with us. She also scheduled a belly dancing performance, and we did attend. I immediately understood why Maddie looked so relaxed and content after each massage therapy, because her therapist performed dances revealing a sensitivity and awareness of every nerve, muscle, and feeling that she had. She involved her complete being both spiritual and physical, and the result was an experience that I rejoiced our Maddie Mae had known.

We even added an overlay on Maddie's mattress that conformed to her shape and facilitated Maddie's condition of immobility. More and more comfort from caring people replaced any burden before it occurred. Hospice workers altered some of Maddie's clothes to prevent unanticipated results in dressing her. Long sleeved dresses were next to impossible, but with the sleeves made short the difficulty was eliminated. Hospice volunteers installed a special shower head to diminish the difficulty of Maddie's bath (for her mother). Laura would place Maddie on her bath seat, and then use the shower head to hose the water on her body and hair. Hospice also had a social worker who visited Maddie regularly. She far surpassed any expectations of her job. She found a group of musicians who would write, perform, and tape a song capturing events, feelings, people, and descriptions of moments in Maddie's life too special to ever loose. When our social worker brought the CD, titled Maddie's Song, the intensity of our feelings when it was played was overwhelming. I still play the song and cry of course. They included all of us involved in Maddie's daily routine and the special edition each one of us was to her life. The song ended with the words, "The world's most beautiful girl, Madison we love you." Maddie's social worker was also instrumental in having the Make A Wish foundation include Maddie in the exclusive gift of a trip to Walt Disney World for Maddie and her family. It was the most memorable time, and once again it made me so mindful of all the goodness in this world in response to adversity. Two representatives arrived at our home with balloons, pizza for the family, and a Winnie the Pooh tape and bear because Maddie loved Winnie the Pooh.

Don't anyone touch my pooh

We got her a musical Winnie the Pooh that would play song after song and calm her to sleep if she were struggling at all with her secretions. When we buried Maddie, we put the raggedy almost four year old Pooh right at her head because he was always with her whether in hospitals, or on trips, and always at home. We did not buy her a new one because there was something special about the one that she had. The Make A Wish foundation was completely instrumental in orchestrating a trip where we had nothing to do at all but show up and enjoy every second of the enchantment, fantasy, entertainment, and recognition that "Maddie You Are Very Special".

I'm not sure about this bear!

Disney had a smaller mouse, more my style

My Aunt Valory thinks I'm the cat's pajamas

My oldest daughter, Valory, had a friend that had previously worked for Make A Wish; and he also knew many people at the Cincinnati Hospital, so he was constantly being a facilitator and availing himself always when problems occurred. When we had Maddie baptized, we named him Maddie's godfather and Laura's sister, Valory, of course was Maddie's godmother. Her godfather never missed any event pertaining to Maddie. His goodness enriched her life tremendously. For her birthdays he would always select a gift that Laura and I had never seen, and yet it would perfectly meet some of Maddie's special needs. Of course, I will have to mention here that he gave Maddie's brother a drum set that nearly ended our friendship. Because he did not have kids of his own, he was not quite aware of the annoyances that follow a loud electric drum set. For her fourth birthday, he had found a mat covered in soothing soft material that massaged in different levels and directions and even had music. Maddie loved music. She listened to CD's that were given to her by many different friends. There were always many strangers who came to meet this loving child; and she would change any one's attitude and feelings about life, even after a short encounter with Miss Maddie. You could see her determination and courage to remain in her environment even though it was encumbered with equipment, medicines, and difficulties. All Maddie desired was to receive and give all the abundant love she brought from heaven. That was Maddie's gift.

Hospice provided us with a sitter three times a week, so we could run errands. Laura and I both always had our cell phones because Maddie could become compromised at any moment. We were so vigilant with her. There were two different Hospice sitters, and both of them embraced her with different and unimaginable ways. They were inspired with the love that they got back as Maddie batted her beautiful eyes three times whenever she saw them. They both found creative ways to calm and soothe Maddie if she was experiencing anxiety close to medicine times. They read to her and created new hairstyles for her that were so unique and beautiful. Hospice would also arrange for a special sitter if emergency needs arose.

When I first moved to Lexington, I dislocated my elbow; and even after it was put back in place, it continued to dislocate. I finally found that I could fix it myself just enduring a little pain. I simply would not have surgery and leave Laura alone with Maddie and Taylor. I finally found an excellent doctor who performed a very lengthy and tedious surgery and agreed to let me go home with Laura as soon as I awoke. I was not much physical help, but at least my love and support of my family was back with them. We really were a good team, and I completely understand why I was forced to retire and move to Lexington. It was all part of a plan, a bigger picture, and the development of a complete dependency on God. I did learn once and for all that I am in control of nothing. There is a serene sense of comfort and confidence with this knowledge. Another area of Hospice involvement was the availability of a nurse all night if an emergency occurred. Maddie could be fine one moment, and then her secretions would tighten cutting off her air flow. If we needed someone to listen to her lower bases, they were quickly available. Laura also had a wonderful neighbor who was a nurse; and during the day, if Laura felt that Maddie was not breathing deeply enough or not often enough, her friend would come over very quickly and listen to Maddie's breathing. For the four miraculous years of Maddie's life, we were so inspired as we encountered the human spirit of so many and the goodness evoked in response to Maddie's love. There was a family in Laura's neighborhood that heard the heart felt story of Maddie, and the mother began stopping by Laura's house with food at first, and then a friendship evolved, and finally she became one of Laura's greatest supporters. She had a heated pool, and Laura and Maddie were invited frequently to share in the pleasure of a swim with friends. Her generosity, however, continued to add sunshine to our lives; and she even shared her God given talents and abilities and created a calendar for my mother, Maddie's great grandmother. It was not an ordinary calendar but one that included many pictures of her children, grandchildren and great grandchildren. It was a treasure for my mother, since she lived in Atlanta and was never able to see us. Arthritis had made my mother's life very difficult, but that calendar filled with her family eased some late nights when pain was compromising her ability to sleep. When our friend lost a family member, she even shared her pulse ox machine for our monitoring of Maddie's oxygen saturation; and she altered Maddie's third year birthday dress. What a spirit filled friend!!!!! Another lady, whom I never met, reached out to me and left a memory and story that I love to tell. Laura and I were browsing in this specialty shop one day after Maddie had joined her father in heaven. I noticed these beautiful bracelets made with crystals and beads that you could tailor design, choosing how many strands, the color and any message. I decided immediately to order a bracelet made with three strands using pink crystals and silver square beads; and each strand spelled one word in my message, "Maddie My Love". When I was called to pick up the bracelet, the lady who had handcrafted it also left a wrapped box. She had heard the story of our brave little girl, and she sent the matching earrings as her response of a blessing to our family. I wear my Maddie jewelry everyday in deepest appreciation. This lovely lady had included a note sharing her same heartfelt grief for a child that she had lost.

Our air conditioning system failed in the hottest part of the summer when Maddie was three. We called for a repair man found in the phone book, and he came immediately on a Sunday. He just added coolant and changed our filter. Unfortunately several weekends later, the air conditioning shut down again; and it was on the weekend. Once again we called the same repair man, but he said that the diagnosis was much more complicated and very expensive. I thanked him for coming and explained that our funds were limited and had to be utilized for the special needs of our little Maddie. When he asked if she was on Hospice; and I said yes, another wonderful person graced our life. He said that our system would be fixed at no cost, and that his mother was an angel like Maddie; but in a different way. His mother volunteered for Hospice and would sit with the terminally ill who were in their last hours and had no one to be with them as they departed. The young man did fix our air conditioning, and he would not be compensated with any money from us. He met Maddie and said, "there is not much I can do for Maddie, but I can do this for the family". Once again, the love poured out for one special little girl reinforced my original urge to write this book. I also wrote Hospice about the generosity of this young man; and I told them that his mother was one of their own, nurturing life abundant for anyone in need. Hospice to me is not considered the end of the road, but rather a new beginning.

This is some of the family surrounding me with love

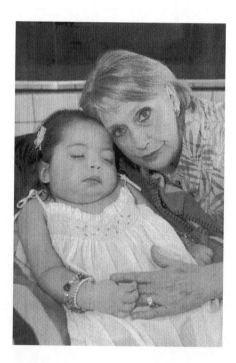

My Gagee & I have such unique times, but she really can't sing

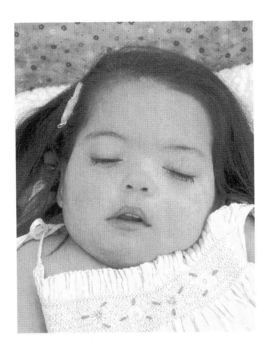

Want to see an angel? Just look!

Maddie's third year had its ups and downs. She did have to be hospital-
ized the day before Halloween, but her mother did not let that deter
her from bringing Maddie's duck costume and putting it on her. I have
to say, even if I am the grandmother, she was the cutest duck ever. The
nurses enjoyed her so much. They brought people into her room to
share in this beautiful child's embracing of life even when death could
soon be approaching. Maddie did return home this time, however; and
we continued reveling in her presence with us everyday that we had
her. Support continued to make its presence, and the school system
sent two preschool teachers to work with Maddie once a week. We had
no idea how creative two human beings could be in a sincere effort to
enhance the life of a terminally ill child embracing life in a limited
environment. These two teachers read to Maddie, brought puppets to
accompany their stories, made hand prints for her mother to cherish
always; and they held her hand so that she could create her very own

art work to be displayed in her room. Our gratitude for their willingness to extend so much of themselves in the endeavor was greater than
words could express.

More family surrounding me with love

Most people have an appreciation for family, but our entire family
with members living in multitudinous places provided a support system that truly sustained us.

Granddaddy, what big hands you have

We received packages, cards, emails, and letters with words of encouragement on a regular basis. I believe that Maddie's development her first ten months being so normal, and then everyone having to watch or hear as she lost all of her abilities and endured increasing pain, created an impact that was so unfamiliar to our family. Each one responded differently to this sadness. Each response was an outpouring of emotions that might have remained still and quiet and never been expressed; and yet the feelings behind those emotions stood for a family bond and dedication that was stronger than anyone of us had realized before. Once again, I found joy in sadness and beauty in devastation. And in the middle of this family bond of support was a very special bond between three children that proffered from time to time a love and understanding of life that most of us never experience.

This is a band that will never be broken

Taylor (Laura's son) and Regan (Valory's daughter) and Maddie (Laura's Angel) shared spoken and unspoken feelings of love and appreciation for each other that would leave all of them different when they had to tell Maddie goodbye for right now. Their closeness when Maddie was here was so inspirational to watch. Taylor and Regan would get up in Maddie's bed with her and play with her in such a childlike manner. She watched, enjoyed, and even batted those beautiful eyes to add her words of love. Now when Taylor and Regan ride in the car with me, they want to sing the Maddie's songs from her funeral service (The music from the DVD of her life). They particularly love You Light Up My Life, The Itsy Bitsy Spider, The Dance, and they belt out, You Raise Me Up. I can never control my tears when those two are in the backseat just rejoicing in God's gift, Maddie Mae. When Regan comes to town, because she and her mother live in Cincinnati now; she always wants to go to the cemetery and leave something there for Maddie. On one trip back from Cincinnati, we stopped to get gas for the car. I went in to get Regan a drink. This old store had a big locked cabinet in the corner filled with crystals. Regan immediately found a crystal of two small bears, one with pink eyes and the other with blue eyes sharing one big red heart between them. She wanted me to get that for Maddie to take to the cemetery, because it reminded her of Taylor and his little sis. Of course we got that one and many others as we journeyed back and forth. When I would take Regan shopping, she would always get distracted by something so perfect for Maddie. What selflessness for a four year old child!!!! Those two children reflected the most beautiful gift sent from heaven named Angel Maddie. Taylor and Regan realized what a blessing life is; and they developed a completely different level of sensitivity, compassion, empathy, and understanding that will impact their life's direction and meaningfulness forever.

We celebrated Maddie's birthday the 16th of every month. Her actual birthday was July 16th; but we wanted her to experience the celebration of her birth as much as possible, since we never knew when God would

call Maddie back home. We sang to her first thing on the 16th of each
month, and I had purchased the cutest little birthday dog that danced
and sang Happy Birthday to You. Maddie always batted her eyes at her
dog. This year we are planning to celebrate her life at the cemetery. I
suggested that we bring her birthday dog. Taylor, Maddie's brother,
reminded us that we had placed her very important dog in her casket. I
remembered, however, that when I bought the little dog for Maddie,
Taylor was mad that he was overlooked. Well you better believe that
within the hour there was another birthday dog. I do not think that he
ever used his birthday dog, but at least we have one now for our celebration. No matter what the dynamics of your family might be, there is
one guarantee—that sibling rivalry will always prevail. Laura had a
good friend who permitted her special gift to resurface in her response
to Maddie. She had for years created the most decorative and delecta-
ble cakes ever. They were a work of art. She had retired completely,
however, from cake making to focusing on motherhood. We were so
thrilled when she told Laura to select her accessories for Maddie's first
birthday party, and she would design a cake to match. The appearance
and taste of that cake embodied a unique experience because it was the
expression of a human spirit reaching out to impact our special little
girl's life. She became known as the cake lady; but she did not create
any other cakes except Maddie's, for all four birthdays. Each cake was
the most overwhelmingly beautiful creation I have ever seen. The cakes
were so special, and everyone that was privileged to experience her cre-
ations commented on how they were of divine inspiration. They had to
be.

All of my birthday cakes could win a competition…1st place

Tied for 1st place

Another...tied for 1st place

Say it with me, another tied for 1st place

I'm four and so loved

Maddie's 4th birthday party

Soon after Maddie's fourth birthday party, which was celebrated at Gattitown because Maddie could ride the carousel with her mother and watch the big screen television; Laura and I both felt a sense of urgency to plan another trip for Maddie Mae. We knew that it was not feasible to go too far away, so we searched the internet and selected Dollywood. Our plans began falling into place, and it gave us something to talk about with both children and to create an environment of excitement anticipating this experience. Usually the anticipation is as exciting as the actual event. Unlike our trip to Disney World, it did take a lot of preparation for this trip; and the momentum rose until it was time to depart. The van looked like a space mobile ready to launch. All we needed was Chevy Chase and the movie cameras could begin rolling to make another in his series, "Vacation" movies. We had searched the internet for appropriate housing because it was mandatory to keep Maddie in as sterile and sanitary environment as possible. Well, we learned the hard way the actuality of what you see and read on the internet and what you truly may encounter in person might be extremely different. We found on the internet this beautiful lodge with mountains behind it, and serene with a heated pool filled with crystal clear water. When we arrived at our anticipated destination, we all had a look of horror on our faces. I do not know; but the mountains must have fallen down, the pool looked like scum or mold was all that could possibly swim in it and the little deck rails and chairs outside each room were covered in rust. We never even turned off the ignition.

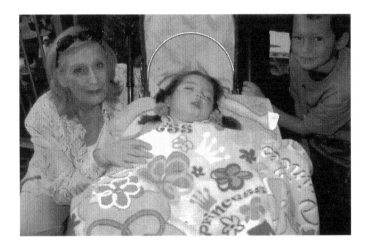

My Gagee sharing Dollywood with me. What fun!

We just found another place that was suitable and had a heated indoor pool which Maddie loved. This pool was different from our hot tub or the YMCA that would allow her water therapy only at special times. This pool came equipped with children, and you could see how much she loved watching them play and have fun. She could also enjoy engaging in play with her brother, or interacting in a childlike environment. I know that our little Maddie Mae is playing now also, after first gracing this world, and leaving it such a better place. My heart broke that day in the pool. Her little face was completely illuminated with joy. Laura and I really learned a very important lesson about life. You can make life warm, happy, cozy and desirous even for a terminally ill child. That would be my message to the doctor who said four years ago, when I asked him, "How can we enhance the quality of Maddie's life?" His response, "Quality? There will be no quality!!! because there will be no longevity." Maddie left this world fighting for life and to remain here, and that is symbolic of a child who has experienced quality of life and shared her gifts and made her impact on many, wrapped in a blanket of our love.

Wrapped in a blanket of love

Maddie's last day had been very routine and without any warnings. Her Hospice nurse had made her normal visit to listen to her lungs. She said, "Maddie is real junky in her upper airway, but that is just secretions. She is moving air great in her lower bases." That was important!!! The day progressed, and she then had her weekly therapy session with her physical therapist. Her therapist had brought over her little orthodics that were made for Maddie in order to sustain the positioning of her feet. Her therapist did not want her heels to drop.

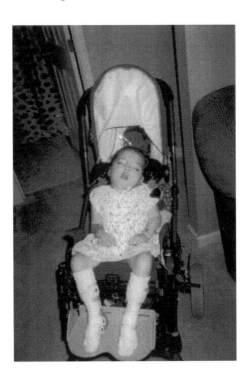

My orthodics were neat. Just another expression of love

The orthodics were made by this company free of charge. Her therapist had taken a picture of Maddie in her new orthodics. So many people were kind in donating life enhancers and their talents. Maddie's second year and third year birthday pictures were taken by a gifted photographer, Cheryl Flora, with a big heart. Her name was given to Laura by a friend of hers that had previously lost her child to this horrible disease, Krabbe. The photographer traveled many miles to offer her love and talents. For her second birthday, a friend that had also lost a child with Krabbe attended Maddie's second year birthday party. She brought Maddie a charm bracelet with her name inscribed on a purse charm that was surrounded by tiny diamonds. Every occasion we always bought Maddie a charm to go on her very special bracelet. It came from a very dear friend that had experienced embracing the love of a child with Krabbe.

That night we prepared for our normal nightly routine, and Taylor was at his Dad's which proved to be very fortunate timing for his visit. I was going to take the 11:00 pm shift, giving Maddie her medicines, checking for absorption, and suctioning her when she had absorbed her medicines, and then beginning her feeding—then the best part of all, holding her little hand until falling peacefully asleep. I awoke a little before 3:00 am; and I checked her oxygen, and it was low. I then called for her mother, and she phoned Hospice; but then she cancelled because Maddie's Oxygen began to elevate as her mother suctioned and then used some percussion to loosen the secretions. Her oxygen elevated again, and she seemed fine. Her mother performed her 3:00 am regimen, and then they fell asleep. For some reason Laura awoke, and Maddie was losing oxygen quickly. She screamed for me to dial 911. The paramedics arrived but did not realize that Maddie could have a secretion plug that deep suctioning could remove; and since she was on Hospice, they were indifferent. Laura did ask them to deep suction her, but her mouth was too dry. Laura then suggested that they use saline while deep suctioning. They got some secretions out but not enough. They intubated her at the hospital and attempted to get a breath, but they declared her deceased. Laura and I were unable to leave her. We could not let go, and so they pulled a curtain around us. This very kind lady came to us and said, "I know that I cannot help the devastation that you are feeling, but I do want you to know that there is not one dry eye on this floor." Yes, our little Maddie had reached so many people and in so many ways; and she looked like an angel. Laura and I were holding her, and she took three deep breaths. Each time we screamed for a doctor. Finally, a doctor said, "these are just reflexes, and he left." However, God had the last word; and Maddie batted those gorgeous big eyes three times. We knew this was not the end. She was telling us goodbye for now.

Our funeral home let Laura and me remain as long as we wanted dressing, adorning, and loving our Maddie. We could visit over the period of two days as long as we needed, and we took total advantage of this time that supplied memories to treasure. The funeral home that you select is so important, because the devastation accompanying the loss of a loved one renders you unable to make any decisions for the viewing and funeral. The only thought that I had was to take my daughter, Laura, to her favorite children's store with the most exclusive dresses ever. We could never buy a dress there before, because they all had buttons or bows or sashes which Maddie could not wear without adverse effects. I told Laura to pick out any dress that she envisioned equal to the beauty of her Maddie. I reminded her that she did not have to consider any health hazards whatsoever. Maddie can now have the most beautiful dress there. Believe me, Laura found the most angelic, gorgeous, and heavenly inspired creation for her little girl; and she also purchased matching bows to put on her braided hair and a bracelet to match her dress. I had given Maddie a beautiful diamond cross for her second Christmas, but the sterling silver chain irritated her neck, so I had to buy a smaller chain to make it a bracelet. Now I could replace this chain with the original chain; and Maddie wore her cross as a necklace for all to see, God's angel!

Maddie's service was completely heart touching. There were two videos playing—one celebrating the joy of her first ten months unencumbered with any apparent disease. Watching these moments of this beautiful child responding to all the love surrounding her, this was a vision of earthly happiness. Then came the glorious moments of a life meant to glorify God, ultimately though in its own unique way; and so she did with a grace never to be forgotten. The Eulogy was delivered by Maddie's godmother and aunt, Valory. The last paragraph were my final words which Valory delivered for me—my words of gratitude for the four years God let me love and enjoy my angel. From this point on, the actual funeral I cannot recreate, because it is though it did not happen. My one and only memory is the singing of Jesus Loves Me which I requested because that was one of our everyday morning songs, the one that she batted her eyes all the way through. I believe that the Lord wants my memories to terminate with the vision of his Angel here on earth accomplishing her mission of Love "When God Sends An Angel".

We saved the blanket that surrounded Maddie in her final moments. It still has her smell on it. We refuse to wash it a year later. It seems like it is another way to keep her close to us. The bracelet that was given to Maddie on her second birthday, Laura had a few links added to fit her wrist. The jewelry store also knew what devastation had taken place and added the links free of charge. Laura wears Maddie's charm bracelet everyday feeling the connection to her daughter that it supplies. Laura designed Maddie's headstone, and she envisioned it in stained glass. She went to one headstone business here in Lexington, and they recommended another place in Louisville that was more experienced and had a greater selection of stained glass from which to choose. When we arrived at the store, the owner welcomed us and asked to preview Laura's design. He could immediately see the outpouring of love for Maddie by her mother, and he was inspired. As the two of them sat down to create Maddie's stained glass portion of her headstone, it was an overwhelming experience to see a creation take form from the inception of feelings of love and transformed into a work of art. They began with the theme reflecting the beauty and inspiration of Maddie's life. There were to be beautiful mountains with a sun rising from behind and a beautiful rainbow resplendent with its vibrant colors. Three breath taking butterflies were flying through the rainbow, since butterflies were one of Maddie's signature favorites. The inscription read: Maddie Mae, fly high with our hearts. The last decision was the selection of the colors to combine creating a vision that you would never forget once seen. When we were called back to Louisville several months later to view the finished product before it was sealed, it had been placed in the window of the store. The sun shone through it, and we both knew that our eyes would never behold a vision more grasping or compelling then Maddie's stained glass.

Laura planned a service at the cemetery for this July 16th in celebration of Maddie's fifth birthday. She ordered 18 helium balloons for the children to let go and fly high. Attached to the balloons was a beautiful laminated picture of Maddie and her mommy and a note stating, "I am sending these balloons to heaven for my angel's fifth birthday, if they do not reach her in the heavens and are found here on earth, please sign her guestbook." She had attached her website address to the laminated picture. We all wonder if they made it to Maddie. We watched them pass over birds, a plane, and many clouds. All of us circled around and held hands and issued prayers. All I could think of was being asked by people aren't you angry that God took Maddie??? As I stood there holding hands and thinking back on the complete transformation of my life because of this child, I emphatically replied, "No with a big!!!! I am so thankful God gave us Maddie and shared with us a small piece of Heaven."

My 5th birthday was in Heaven, but not forgotten on earth

Now a little over one year later since Maddie's departure, there is not one day that does not claim some of my tears; but some are of sadness and loss, and others are of joy. Everyone experiences tears of sadness; but the tears of joy from Maddie, they have left me a vessel just ready to share God's love everywhere. Life as I know it now is so beautiful, just like my precious angel, Maddie Mae. Even though my heart aches everyday for her, I will perpetuate Maddie's purpose, a selfless love like no other except for God's. "To God be the glory for the great things he hath done."

Maddie, Val and Regan at Christmas

Maddie's Eulogy written by my daughter Valory, Maddie's Aunt

The gates of Heaven opened wide when God gave us Maddie. We are here today to celebrate her life. Maddie was the epitome of a perfect little girl: The largest of brown eyes, a head of thick beautiful dark hair, and a heart of the purest of gold. She had a smile that would make you believe that this world was a perfect place and help you rejoice in the things in life we thought not possible. Life isn't created by words. It is created by actions. Maddie was a vessel of God's love and through her mere presence was an incredible declaration of the love she had for life. A mother's love is said to be the strongest love of all. The sound of Laura's voice would light up Maddie's face like nothing else. Laura began each day with such love and optimism. She was determined not only to get through each day, but to take the time to pick out the most precious outfits and accessories. She painted Maddie's fingernails and toenails to match each outfit. We showed Maddie each day how beautiful she looked. Laura was so in tune with everything in Maddie's life from keeping her schedule with all of her medicines to picking up on infections before the medical test could even detect them.

She kept their calendar full of fun. There was not a week that passed with out something fun planned for the children. There was a trip to Disneyland, the aquarium, the zoo, the park, the pool, anything and everything she could think of, although plans were subject to change according to how Maddie was feeling. This gave the children something to anticipate. My sister truly understood that each day Maddie was with us was a gift. It was Maddie's gift.

My mother, Maddie's Gagee, was the other half of this team that made it possible for this family to thrive. She began each day with a puppet show (I have witnessed these and trust me, words could not describe them). She then continued throughout the day with reading Maddie's favorite books and singing Maddie's favorite songs. Her selfless dedication to Laura, Maddie, and Taylor was reflective in her impeccable care of her family. Yet, as arduous a lifestyle as it was, you would not hear a complaint because it was done out of love. Friends who came to visit would walk away in awe over the manner in which they kept the family going as smoothly as they did in spite of ongoing obstacles. It was inspirational and courageous, a true definition of unconditional love.

Maddie 2nd Christmas with mommy and Gagee

I bring out the weirdness in my brother

Halloween can be real scary

Taylor is the best brother. I just have to be prepared for some of his antics

Taylor was such a wonderful big brother. He had to have been so confused with all that was happening. Taylor's mom and dad worked well with one another to keep him as busy as any other little boy. They kept him in soccer and T-Ball and helped stay on top of his studies, but he was young to have to process what was going on around him. "What are all these machines in our house?" "Who are all these nurses and therapists?" "Why can't Maddie eat with her mouth?" "Mommy do you think Maddie will be able to walk when she is 5?" Maddie required so much time and care, but Taylor never complained. He was a loving, wonderful, compassionate big brother. Not a day passed without a kiss on the forehead and a hug around her neck. He is an amazing little boy!!!

My bother watches over me...always

Maddie loved her Dad. He planned special trips with Taylor and Maddie and came over to see her each week. His love truly showed through his determination to get the newborn screening approved. He spent a great amount of time on this cause to help families with sick children give them a chance to survive this illness. This is a wonderful cause.

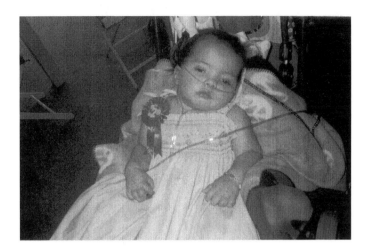

I'm 2 and beautiful. God created me!

Maddie was with us far longer than anyone would have imagined. She defied every prognosis. Laura was faced constantly with people who did not share her same optimism on Maddie's life, who couldn't see past her shell and know she was fighting each day because of the love that surrounded her. Through her strength and determination for life she proved the doctors to have no understanding of a God given human spirit. When Maddie was diagnosed her mother asked, "How long do you think that we will have Maddie?" His response was, "She will most likely not see her second birthday." Oh! How Maddie proved him so very wrong!! Any and everybody that was part of her life could see that special light that showed through in Maddie. She had so many people that loved her, and she touched so many lives. Her massage therapist and physical therapist were incredible with her, helping her muscles stay stretched and her body moving was very beneficial to her. Her teachers that came to read to her, and her Hospice nurses that came to check on her. Everyone saw the special quality that was the essence of

Maddie. The ripple effect of her mark here on earth will continue for years to come.

When I think of Maddie, the word faith comes to mind. She showed people that did not understand the meaning of this word, what faith was all about. She fought very hard each day to get to the next, but why?? She could not run and play with her brother or friends. She could not ask her mother questions. She could not communicate the way other children did so she used her eyes. A simple batting twice of her eyes to answer yes she was ok was as calming as any word could have ever been....And to be as blessed as to get BAT, BAT, BAT (which meant I Love You) was a blessing like no other. So how does faith take a part in Maddie's life? I believe it does by knowing that as blessed as we were to have her every moment we did, and as special as each bat of her eyes was, we now have solace in knowing that she is in a place where she can skip and jump and sing and play. She can do all the things she was not able to do here.

I would like to take a moment and share with you some thoughts from Maddie's Gagee, my mother: "Well once again the Heavens have opened wide, and God has taken Maddie back home with him. But to Laura and Maddie, I'm sure God is saying, "Job well done my daughters!" The value of life cannot be measured by time on earth but rather by its significance on the lives of others. Maddie with her quiet, gentle, soft touch on life has proffered to many the very essence of our time on earth. It is not worldly goods or capabilities that define and nurture our human spirit; because Maddie lost all her physical abilities one at a time, until she appeared to have no reason to live. It was, however, from this assumed lifeless state that she grew and flourished for years longer than any doctor said possible. And she epitomized life's foremost lesson that the one and only common thread necessary for quality life or life at all is to Love and be Loved....And Maddie is so Loved."

Thank You, God, for our Maddie Mae

My mommy knows how to make life great

Laura wrote a journal entry On August 21st, two days after we lost Maddie.

Words cannot describe how I am feeling. I have to say sad, lost, and my heart is broken into a million pieces. My Maddie was my world and my life. I long for one last smell, and touch, and holding of her sweet hand. I am so confused about what happened. I know that people think because she has been on Hospice for three years that I should be prepared. I am not nor could I have ever prepared myself for the hole that is missing from my heart. I wake up at three in the morning knowing it is time for the medicine, catheterizing; and the only problem is that there is no Maddie. Maddie slept in bed with me. She had her feeding pump on one side and her suction machine tucked behind the pillows to prevent the banging of the machine on the headboard. I have not heard the sound of the suction machine being turned on, and the oxygen machine making its usual hum. My house is so silent. We went yesterday to dress Maddie at the funeral home, and I had a hard time leaving her. I gave her thousands of kisses and held her hand so tight. I braided her hair like I do everyday. I also put body glitter all over her body, and put her usual lip gloss that moistens her lips just right. I repainted her purple nails and toes pink. Purple does not match with a pink dress. My mom and I picked out her beautiful dress. Maddie had a multitude of polishes along with hair accessories. Her lip glosses were either colored or even some had glitter in them. Believe me, she looked like a beauty queen everyday!!!!

That night is played over in my head like a bad dream; and I wish that I had not called 911, so that I could have had those last special moments with my Maddie. I wanted to hold her, but I couldn't while they worked so hard to bring her back. I was not ready nor would I have ever been ready. I took such pride in dressing Maddie to perfection and handling her healthcare. I feel like if I had just had a warning. I remember asking Maddie's nurse if I will have signs that the end is near. She had mentioned that there would be signs. One of the big signs that we always checked was her absorption. It was important that she continue to absorb medicine and food. If she ever started to slow down with her absorption, it would throw me into a panic mode.

Last weekend we went to the Newport Aquarium in Cincinnati. We then went to the movies the next day. Maddie did great all weekend. Maddie had not been sick. Her Hospice nurse had stopped by on late Thursday afternoon and commented on the fact that she was a little junky, but she had good air movement. Maddie also had her usual physical therapy session that day. Everything seemed to be normal. That night around midnight, I called Hospice and notified them that her oxygen level was low. While I was on the phone with them, I got it back up, so I told them never mind. She is doing okay!!! Around 3:00 am I checked her stats, and they had gone back down. I suctioned, and her oxygen went back up. I had listened to her earlier, and she appeared to be moving air in her bases, so I was not too concerned. I fell asleep while her albuterol treatment was running, and suddenly I awoke. I checked her oxygen level. It was real low. I screamed for my mom in the other room. I told her to call 911. I knew it was a plug and it needed to come out. The paramedics arrived and were very insensitive. They said, "she is barely breathing. What do you want us to do?" I replied, take her to the hospital!!! They had announced since she was a Hospice patient they were unsure of what to do. I explained that this had happened in the past. It is a plug blocking her airway. She is not able to get any oxygen. Her mouth was so dry. I couldn't help but be totally frustrated with their lack of concern, since she was on Hospice. I told the paramedic that I use saline before I suction when her mouth gets dry. I really felt like we would never get to the hospital. Every minute was crucial. The ambulance driver got lost in my neighborhood. My mom was sitting up front and had to redirect them. We were losing more time. When we arrived at the Emergency Room, they were not aware of the severity of her condition. The doctors were yelling at the Paramedics asking them at what point did she decline. They were unsure. At that moment, they were sticking her everywhere and increasing the amounts of epinephrine in order to get her heart beating again. They worked on reviving Maddie for about twenty minutes. All I think of is that I wanted them to quit sticking her. I just wanted to hold her. They pronounced her deceased at 6:30 am. I asked them to remove all the wires, so that I could hold her tight. My mom then held her also. Maddie took several breaths. We called for the doctors to come over. They said it was just her reflexes. While my mom was holding her, she batted her eyes three last times. It was as if she was saying goodbye for now. I really think that was her way of letting us know that she had arrived at a better place. I know she is in heaven, but I want her here with me. I miss her so much. I know God gave me Maddie because he knew that I would take the best care of her, but it was not enough. I know her Hospice nurse will probably never forget the time that I paged her in a total panic. She wanted to know if Maddie was okay. I told her that I cut her beautiful hair, and that it looks awful. She said, "We have a volunteer that cuts hair. I will get her out to fix Maddie's hair." Knowing me, patience is not my forte. I took her to a kids cutting place to have it fixed immediately. Believe me Maddie's nurse had heard it all.

We went to Dollywood in July and had the best vacation. Maddie's life would have not been the same without the love from all of you. Maddie's Gagee, my mom, stayed with me every night so that we could make her life the very best. We played so many musical beds that it would make your head spin. Mom started out with Maddie from 11:00pm-3:00am. She would then lay out the medicines that I had prepared before we went to bed. I would in and out catherize and give her the medicines. I typically had to wait a while for the medicines to be absorbed before I could hook her back up to her continuous feed. I would watch many hours of television, and typically fall asleep with my glasses still on, and the TV full blast, and all of the lights still on. It was a circus, but it worked. I am also thankful for all that Maddie's daddy did for the newborn screening. I never wanted to seem disinterested, but I just did not want to take Maddie out into the public. I know I may have tried to keep her in a bubble, but I took pride in trying to keep her away from any illnesses. I Love You, Maddie. You will never know what an impact your short life made on so many people. It is seeing Maddie for who she is, not seeing the horrible disease. I Love You, my sweet angel. Have fun in heaven and make sure and give your Great Grandpa a big kiss from your mommy!!!!!

Love,
Laura (Maddie's mommy)

Christmas is a special birthday that we all celebrate

What family will do for you

Taylor and Maddie 2nd Christmas

Maddie, Taylor and Mommy 3rd Christmas

My gagee spends every second with me

I wrote a journal entry to Maddie on January 18th.

A letter from Grandma (Gagee)

To my precious angel Maddie. It has been nearly five months since you flew high with our hearts, and I now know that the pain of losing you will never lessen; but the love and joy that you gave us has become a metamorphosis of that pain, just like the caterpillar into your signature butterfly. I look back over your four short years and wonder how can I possibly follow in your footsteps. In the midst of what appeared to be such sadness, you radiated true beauty and love and the real meaning of life without any possessions or abilities that imprison us. You had nothing, or so it appeared; but you gave everything, and this world took on a new appearance. I thank God everyday for honoring us with you; and in his wisdom knowing Laura would manifest a miracle of her own by creating such a special life for Maddie, that she would choose to live much longer than any doctors predicted she could. God gave us many special gifts that far surpassed any earthly experiences. The night I leaned over and said, "Maddie, (blink of my eyes) I (another blink) love (another blink) you." (blink) You blinked back three times. That was a moment never to be forgotten, and it opened the door of communication that grew and grew and allowed us to know that our hearts were beating in unison. We did know and love each other. The last time, that your precious blinks stopped our hearts, was the night that they pronounced you deceased; and after that pronouncement, by God's great glory, you blinked those heart rendering big eyes three times which let us know death had not separated us. Maddie I am glad that I do not have too many years left to try and be reflective of all I learned from you. I cannot wait to meet you at the Golden Gates. I love you more because of the real definition of Love that I learned from you.

Your adoring Gagee.

978-0-595-41502-1
0-595-41502-4

5074097R0

Made in the USA
Lexington, KY
31 March 2010